DO YOUR JOB

THE LEADERSHIP PRINCIPLES THAT BILL BELICHICK AND THE PATRIOT HAVE USED TO BECOME THE BEST DYNASTY IN THE NFL

Presented By:

LESSONS IN LEADERSHIP INSTITUTE

LessonsInLeadership.Institute

Copyright © 2018

INTRODUCTION

Do Your Job, this simple, universal saying has come to define the culture of the most successful sports dynasty in America. In this book you will learn the origins and applications of the core beliefs that have lead to the greatest dynasty in NFL History.

With a specific focus on the origins and the manifestations of these core principles, this book will show you how to apply the principles that have built a dynasty in New England to your organization.

By chronicling the start of the coaching legend and following through to modern day this book will take you through the main principles that guide Coach Belichick as he makes the decisions for the Patriots. Learn how these lessons can be applied to your life and organization and allow your team to reach new heights.

Take the first step to win the Super Bowl of your industry!

TABLE OF CONTENTS

LEGAL NOTES

Do Your Job: The Leadership Principles that Bill Belichick and the Patriots Have Used to Become the Best Dynasty in the NFL by Lessons in Leadership Institute

THE FOUNDATION OF A LEGACY

Bill Belichick, head football coach of the New England Patriots, has football in his blood. Born William Stephen Belichick in Nashville, Tennessee on April 16, 1952, Belichick was the only child of Jeannette and Steve Belichick. By the time young Bill was born, Steve Belichick had already proven his football savvy.

Steve Belichick, the youngest of five children, was in his teens when the Great Depression hit his home state of Pennsylvania, along with the rest of the country. The Depression left the family without a source of income, and unemployment lines and soup kitchens became the family's salvation. Eventually, Steve Belichick found a job in the Pennsylvania steel mills, but when his mill shuttered its doors, he had one option left – take up his high school teacher's offer of a college football scholarship. Football was Steve Belichick's path out of poverty and unemployment and he viewed the sport as more than just a game. For him, it was serious business – it was his livelihood. He carried this attitude with him as a college player, equipment manager for the Detroit Lions, college football coach, and eventually, a football scout for the United States Naval Academy. He also instilled this attitude in his son, Bill.

Bill Belichick was, from an early age, an observant student of his father's football tutelage. He gained a thorough understanding of the way his father gleaned information about individual players from game film. He watched as his father drew up plays and then implemented them. He attended coaches meetings and team practices and noticed how the relationship between coach and player in the locker room translated on to the field.

As a student at Wesleyan University in Connecticut, Bill Belichick played lacrosse, rather than football, while earning his degree in economics, but football never left him. When he graduated in 1975, he accepted a $25 a week job as a "gopher" for Baltimore Colts head coach, Ted Marchibroda. This was a stepping stone, Belichick knew, for his eventual goal of coaching in the NFL. Shortly after, he started a series of different jobs with various NFL teams, including the Denver Broncos and the Detroit Lions. Just four years after graduating from college, Belichick landed his first coaching job as a special team's coach for the New York Giants. The Giant's organization was a good fit for Belichick. He stayed on for twelve seasons and worked his way up to the defensive coordinator position, under Bill Parcells, the head coach who led the team to two Super Bowl wins.

In 1977, Belichick married Debby Clarke, and the couple has three children together, Amanda, Stephen, and Brian. All three Belichick children played college lacrosse, just like their father. Continuing the Belichick legacy, all are currently coaching. Amanda coaches college lacrosse, while her brothers work for the Patriots franchise. Stephen Belichick is the team's safeties coach, and Brian Belichick transitioned from a scouting assistant to a coaching assistant for the defensive coaches. Bill and Debby Belichick divorced in 2006.

LIFE AS A COACH

Bill Belichick considers Bill Parcells to be a role model and mentor. Parcells first met Belichick when he was a child tagging along with his father, Steve Belichick, on scouting trips. During the 1960s, when Steve Belichick served as the football scout for Navy, Parcells was the football scout for Army. The two often shared film and interacted professionally. Their paths crossed again in 1981, when Parcells accepted the defensive coordinator position with the New York Giants, Bill Belichick was already there, working as a special teams coach and defensive assistant.

Parcells took the younger Belichick under his wing. When Belichick shared his goal of becoming a defensive coach with him, Parcells encouraged him to help with the coaching of the linebackers, and later named him the linebackers coach. In 1983, Parcells became the Giant's head coach. He now had it in his power to let his young protégé oversee the team defense. Under Parcells guidance, Belichick developed his coaching strategies. In 1985, Parcells made it official and offered Belichick, then only 31 years old, the defensive coordinator position.

As a defensive coach, Belichick made good use of the talent of Giant's linebacker, Lawrence Taylor, a future Hall of Famer, and turned the Giant's defense into a dominant force throughout the remainder of the 1980s. Belichick's leadership led to two Giant's Super Bowl wins – in 1987 and 1991 – and his defense placed in the top five of all NFL teams, based on yards and points allowed stats, four out of his six years in New York. It was just after the Giant's 1991 Super bowl victory that the Cleveland Browns owner, Art Modell, hired Belichick as its new head coach. When Belichick left New York for Cleveland, he was saying good-bye to his long-time mentor, Bill Parcells. The separation, as fate would have it, was not a long one.

Belichick's time in Cleveland was tumultuous and brief. His tenure lasted from 1991 to 1995, and he had only one winning season. That year, the 1994 season, the Browns made the playoffs in a wild card round and faced the New England Patriots on New Year's Day, 1995. The 20-13 win over the Patriots gave Belichick his first playoff victory as a head coach. A week later, the Browns lost the Divisional game against the Pittsburgh Steelers, 29-9, ending the team's playoff run and ending the season as the NFL's number one defense for points surrendered per game at 12.8 points per game.

The 1995 season, Belichick's last with the Browns, was marred by controversy. That November, the Cleveland Browns' owner, Art Modell, announced that the team would be moving to Baltimore at the conclusion of the season. He expressed dissatisfaction with the Brown's Stadium and support of the Cleveland people. Not unexpectedly, the announcement was met with opposition from fans, residents, and city leaders in Cleveland. On February 9, 1996, the NFL announced that it had reached an agreement with Modell and the city of Cleveland to allow Cleveland to keep the Browns name (in preparation for a new team to come in for the 1999 season) and for the new Baltimore team to become an expansion team.

Throughout the move, Modell had reportedly assured Belichick that he would be the head coach of the new expansion team in Baltimore, which would eventually be named the Ravens. Yet on February 9, 1996, just one week after the move, Belichick was fired. Although he viewed his first head coaching position as a learning experience that helped him to develop more effective coaching strategies, his record with the Browns was only 36-44.

Bill Parcells was quick to scoop up the newly-unemployed Belichick. He joined Parcells' coaching staff of the New England Patriots as the defensive backs coach for the 1996 season. Under the leadership of head coach Parcells, Belichick and the Patriots advanced to the Super Bowl at the end of the season, but were defeated by the Green Bay Packers. Following this loss, Parcells moved to the head coaching position at the New York Jets and brought Belichick back to New York with him. Belichick's official title with the Jets was defensive coordinator and assistant head coach, but in fact, he was being groomed by Parcells to take over as the Jets head coach. Things didn't quite go as Parcells had planned.

Parcells had it all set with the Jets team management. He would resign as head coach and Belichick would fill the slot. Belichick was named the head coach on January 3, 2000, and a press conference was scheduled for the next day to formally introduce him as the Jets next coach. Belichick used the press conference to make a surprise announcement – he was resigning as the Jets head coach after just one day. He tendered his resignation in the form of a hastily hand written message on notebook paper that read, "I resign as HC of the NYJ." The media was stunned, as was Parcells.

Not long after delivering this bombshell, the New England Patriots announced that Belichick would succeed Pete Carroll, who had been recently fired, as the 12th head coach of the franchise. The Jets and Parcells argued that Belichick was still under contract with the Jets and sought compensation from the Patriots. Paul Tagliabue, the NFL Commissioner, stepped in to mediate the disagreement and broker a deal. In the end, the Patriots agreed to give the Jets a 2000 first-round draft pick for the right to hire Belichick away from his former team.

Although Belichick's rookie year as Patriots head coach was rocky, by year two, Belichick realized he had something special in his young quarterback, Tom Brady, who had replaced the starting quarterback, Drew Bledsoe who was injured earlier in the season. Together, Belichick and Brady took the under-dog New England Patriots to a victory in the 2001 Super Bowl over the heavily-favored St. Louis Rams. This win served as the foundation of the Patriot dynasty that was to come.

Together, Belichick, Brady, and the Patriots formed an unstoppable force. Just two seasons after their first Super Bowl win, the Patriots returned to Super Bowl. They defeated the Carolina Panthers, who were making their first appearance in a Super Bowl, 32-29. The very next year, the Patriots were back at it, winning Super Bowl XXXIX with a 24-21 victory over Terrell Owens and the Philadelphia Eagles.

The accolades for Belichick and the Patriots continued. In all, Belichick amassed five Super Bowl Championships (2002, 2004, 2005, 2015, and 2017) and was named the NFL's Coach of the Year three times (in 2003, 2007, and 2010). The Patriots were named the All-Decade Team for the 2000s. Belichick was the first head coach of an NFL team to reign over a 16-0 regular season team in 2007.

In the last 17 seasons, the Patriots have a regular season record of 214-74-0, making Belichick the winningest coach in Patriots franchise history.

Belichick's playoff record is 27-10 and 5-3 in Super Bowls. Under his coaching, the Patriots have won fifteen division titles – a five year streak from 2003 to 2007 and a nine year consecutive run from 2009-2017. Although Belichick is fortunate to have many outstanding players on his roster, including Tom Brady, the secret to his impressive accomplishments lies with his unique form of leadership.

Principle 1: Total Preparation

A football field is a lot like a battlefield and the game itself is much like a war. It is not uncommon for successful coaches to approach the sport in the same way that a general prepares for battle. For Bill Belichick, the ancient words of Sun Tzu's *The Art of War* adapt well to leadership on the gridiron. In fact, he has a quote by Sun Tzu – "Every battle is won before it is fought"—on the wall of his locker room.

The Art of War is a military guidebook that some people have dubbed "the ultimate guide to winning". Written in the 5th century by the Chinese philosopher and military strategist, Sun Tzu, the book has influenced Eastern and Western military ideology and inspired political and military leaders, business leaders, lawyers, and coaches. Each of the 13 chapters in *The Art of War* focuses on an aspect of war and gives details on how strategic planning can result in a favorable outcome. Although written for the battlefield, the concepts outlined in the book can be easily applied to football, and, in fact, *The Art of War* is a favorite tome of coaches in all sports.

The Sun Tzu quote Belichick has in his Patriots locker room that states "Every battle is won before it is fought" speaks to the coach's core belief in preparedness. Belichick is a student of Sun Tzu's as much as he is a student of the game of football. When Tzu wrote that being well-prepared can make any victory a self-fulfilling prophecy, he was not talking about an athletic event, but Belichick could easily connect this concept to his own strategy.

Belichick is a planner and a preparer, in his life and in coaching. He didn't become a head coach by chance, but by preparing himself for the position. As a youngster tagging along with his father, he learned the fundamentals of the game and observed the human aspect of football. He watched, alongside his father, countless hours of recruitment tapes, learning the mind and the body of athletes. He took every opportunity presented to him to learn more about the game and the strategy for winning. More importantly, he learned from his mistakes. While his firing from the Browns was a set-back, time allowed him to reflect on his tenure in Cleveland. Of that period in his life, Belichick noted that he believes one of his biggest mistakes was not trusting his coaching staff enough to delegate responsibilities to them. He has since altered his coaching style so that he relies on a trusted staff of coaches, freeing him to focus on being the head coach.

This tenacity for preparedness is the first key principle in Sun Tzu's *The Art of War*. In this chapter of the famed military strategist's book, we can find other pearls of wisdom that are evident in Belichick's coaching. When Tzu wrote that a "great commander inspires his people to be in such complete accord with him that they will follow him into battle, regardless of their lives", we can see that Belichick interprets this to mean that a good coach creates an environment where his players and assistants fully trust and believe in him. Sun Tzu's words saying that the "commander projects the virtues of wisdom, courage, benevolence, and discipline onto his soldiers" show also that a good leader or coach inspires his team to be as mentally prepared as they are physically prepared. Lastly, Tzu notes that "the general who wins a battle, makes his calculations in his temple before the battle is fought. The general who loses the battle makes but few calculations beforehand." Belichick knows that it is the preparations, planning, practices, and playmaking that happen prior to game day that are key to victory. In addition to the guidance of Sun Tzu, Belichick has explained that his is inspired by Vince Lombardi's famous quote, "The will to win is not nearly so important as the will to prepare to win."

For Belichick, this means each person on the team, from the coaching staff to the players, must all follow four simple, yet vital, rules: 1) Do your job. 2) Be attentive. 3) Pay attention to details. 4) Put the team first.

Belichick has earned a reputation for preparing his team for a multitude of scenarios. For example, at the start of the 2004 season, Belichick expressed concern about backups for this team's defensive line. If injuries occurred, Belichick feared, the team didn't have a secondary line in place. For a coach like Belichick who is accustomed to preparing for long-range possibilities, this posed a challenge. Fortunately, he knew that his wide receiver, Troy Brown, had occasionally played cornerback in college, so Belichick, in a highly unusual move, worked with Brown on defense. Today's NFL rosters are highly specialized so a player playing both offense and defense almost unheard of. Many people thought Belichick was being overly cautious by preparing Brown for a defensive role, but his preparation proved advantageous. Later that season, the Patriots lost two of their main defensive backs, but Bellchick was ready with a fully-prepared Brown to fill their shoes. Brown was invaluable and even added three interceptions to his stats, making him second in interceptions on the team. This is just one of the many instances when Belichick was able to look long-range and anticipate potential problems, then take early steps so he would be prepared to meet these challenges when they arose.

Belichick expects his players to be as prepared for game day as he is. He has gone so far as to give his players pop quizzes. He has worked hard to establish an environment of learning in the locker room and on the practice field. For example, he believes it is important for every player to have an understanding of the big picture, the overall strategic plan for attacking the game. He feels that players who only focus on their position may miss out on knowing exactly how that role fits into the grand scheme. Often, Belichick will work with defensive players on offensive strategies and with offensive players on defensive strategies. Knowledge, Belichick believes, is the first step in preparedness.

Another one of Sun Tzu's guiding principles states, "If you know the enemy and know yourself, you need not fear the results of a hundred battles." This sentiment is often shortened to the phrase, "know your enemy," which is also attributed to Tzu. Belichick makes it his business to know his enemies, or in this case, his opponents. From his father, a former football scout, he learned the fine art of gleaning information from highlight films and exactly what to look for when watching video of other teams in preparation for battling them on the gridiron. He learned to look at both overarching team dynamics and the nuanced moves of each player. With this knowledge, he is able to anticipate how they will react to various plays.

Having an in-depth knowledge of the opponent proves helpful in every game. Once such example was the 2005 playoff game between the New England Patriots and the Indianapolis Colts, played on January 16. For the first time all season, Colts quarterback Manning, the NFL's most valuable player that season, was unable to connect for a touchdown pass. Belichick and his assistants were able to predict where Manning planned to throw the ball and ramped up coverage in those areas. The 20-3 win the Patriots enjoyed was frustrating to Manning, but serves as a good example of how beneficial it can be if you know your enemy. Belichick continues to make it a priority for his staff and his team to study the opposing team.

Belichick's penchant for gathering information on his football opponents was brought into the spotlight during the 2007 football season in an incident that became known as Spygate. The NFL cited the New England Patriots for videotaping the defensive coach's hand signals during a game against New York Jets on September 9, 2007. The incident forced the league to take a closer look at the rules that were in place for recording opposing teams. In general, it is not considered a violation for one team to record another team's actions on the field or on the bench, but there are roles about where such videotaping is allowed and where is it prohibited. The Patriots were shooting the video from their own bench across the field to the Jets' bench. Belichick argued that, since they were recording the Jets' coaches from their own side of the field and not using the information gleaned from the tapes in that same game, the actions did not break NFL rules. Roger Goodell, the NFL Commissioner, disagreed. He stated that the video recordings "represented a calculated and deliberate attempt to avoid long-standing rules designed to encourage fair play and promote honest competition on the playing field." As punishment for the violation, he ordered Belichick to pay a $500,000 fine – the largest fine in NFL history –and fined the Patriots' organization $250,000. In addition, the Patriots were stripped of their first round draft pick for the 2008 NFL draft. Belichick released a statement to his fans, supporters, and to the media apologizing and admitting his mistake in misinterpreting the NFL rules. Although Belichick incurred some negativity after Spygate, he has weathered the crisis by demonstrating his leadership ability and by sticking to his Tzu-inspired "know your enemy" approach, albeit with a newfound understanding of the rules.

While Belichick is inspired by the ancient writings of Sun Tzu, he also credits Paul Brown, coach of the Cleveland Browns during the 1950s, with elevating the game of football to a thinking man's game. Brown stressed mental and athletic preparedness, and expected his staff and players to perform at their highest level on the practice field, in meetings, and during games. From Brown, Belichick learned that, while preparation is vitally important, a good coach never leaves his game on the practice field. Rather than exhausting his players during practice, a big chunk of the preparation should be mental. A team that is mentally strong and mentally prepared, Belichick believes, has the advantage on game day.

Belichick has read many of the books in his father's library, including the 1952 Bud Wilkinson book, Oklahoma Split T Football. The worn pages of the book and the handwritten notes throughout are a testament to how often both Belichicks have referred to the book. Inside the cover, written in black ink, are the words "To Steve Belichick – with best wishes, Bud Wilkinson." Below it, in blue ink, he continued, "Said Napoleon – "Battles are won by the power of the mind." Belichick may have adopted a cerebral approach to football from Brown, but he carries it further into his coaching style. Many of his players and former players have called Belichick the smartest coach in the NFL. Perhaps it is because he is well read. In addition to the works of Sun Tzu, Belichick has studied numerous books on football and coaching, written by such notable coaches as Vince Lombardi and Knute Rockne.

PRINCIPLE 2: A LACK OF TALENT CAN BE MADE UP FOR WITH HARD WORK

While being knowledgeable of the nuances of the game of football is one aspect of Belichick's success, another part has to do with his people skills. Belichick has the ability to recognize untapped talent, inspired his team, and demonstrate that hard work can be a substitute for uncontrolled raw talent.

Players who have reached the NFL level are all extremely talented athletes, but Belichick looks for something more than athletic prowess when recruiting new players. What he wants are players who are passionate for the game of football and who play for the love of the game. So many talented athletes have lost their passion for the game, but they play college football for the scholarship opportunities and enter the NFL draft with dollar signs in their eyes. Certainly, many NFL players sign lucrative contracts and enjoy a degree of celebrity status…and attractive proposition for many players, especially those who grew up impoverished. Belichick, however, is not interested in players who are seeking fame and fortune. Instead, he wants dedicated, passionate, students of the game to fill his roster.

Belichick's formula for rounding out his roster strikes a fine balance between passion and power, and Belichick is always looking to get his money's worth from a player, a concept that is especially critical in the salary cap era. The NFL salary cap was implemented in 1994 to ensure that no one team could exert their dominance over the rest of the teams by signing the best players to high-dollar salaries. Instead, teams need to keep their accumulative payroll under the cap set by the league. The NFL salary cap fundamentally changed the world of professional football. In the past, players stayed with the same team for several years and, therefore, had the time to learn the team's specific coaching styles, be developed by the coaches into a formidable player, and gain valuable experience. Now, because of the salary cap, teams are forced to cut established, higher-paid players and replace them with inexperienced rookies so that they do not exceed the salary cap. For coaches like Bill Belichick, it means making the best decisions when it comes to draft time.

Belichick's rookie selection process has been called "bottom feeding" by several sports writers. The Patriots don't rely on first picks in the draft. Instead of eying the top talent, Belichick scouts the players that fly under the radar. The wide receivers Belichick looks for are typically smaller in stature, but athletic and aggressive. These types of players may be passed over by other teams because of their lack of size, but Belichick has learned that size is no substitute for heart. For example, Troy Brown, at 5' 10", was an eighth-round draft pick. Also at 5' 10", Julian Edelman was selected by the Patriots in the seventh round. Deion Branch, a second-round pick, is 5' 9". The 5' 9" Wes Welker was traded for a second and seventh round picks. Danny Amendola, at 5' 11" was a free agent signing. A lacrosse player like Belichick, 6' 1" Chris Hogan went undrafted before signing with San Francisco as a free agent in 2011. Belichick acquired him in 2016. Randy Moss is the only superstar wide receiver that the Patriots have had during Belichick's tenure, and he was a fourth-round pick.

The same method of seeking unrecognized talent extends to the Patriots running backs as well, but instead of selecting players late in the draft, Belichick eyes players who are older than college age and who are considered to be in their final years as successful running backs. Corey Dillon was 30 years old when he was acquired by the Patriots; LaGarrette Blount and Antowain Smith were both 29. Both Blount and third-dawn back Dion Lewis were signed as free agents and didn't cost the Patriots any draft picks. The last time Belichick used his first round draft pick on a running back was in 2006 when the Patriots acquired Laurence Maroney. Maroney wasn't the stand-out running back Belichick had hoped for and he was released by the Patriots in 2010. Belichick learned from this experience that the team, as a whole, is better off when he puts his money into other positions and utilizes the existing talents and experiences of older, more experienced running backs.

Belichick has chosen, instead, to wager on offensive players. That is where he devotes the bulk of his draft picks and capital. He uses the offensive players to enhance the arm of his star quarterback, Tom Brady. Both Ben Watson and David Graham were second-round draft picks. Rob Gronkowski came to the Patriots as a second-round pick. Aaron Hernandez was a fourth round selection. Belichick traded a fourth-rough draft pick for Martellus Bennett. Have a strong offensive line filled with players who are both smart and adaptable has been a hallmark of Belichick's winning roster-building strategy.

On the defensive side, Belichick used first-round draft picks to acquire Rob Ninkovich and Dont'a Hightower, both linebackers, but he always keeps his eyes open for a good bargain. Belichick signed cornerback Malcolm Butler as an undrafted free agent because he was so impressed with what he saw in the University of West Alabama player during a post-draft tryout camp. Butler had one of the most memorable plays in Super Bowl history when, during the remaining seconds of Super Bowl XLIX, Butler intercepted a pass at the goal line, preventing the Seattle Seahawks from scoring and ensuring the Patriots' 28-24 victory.

During Super Bowl LII, Butler, who had played in 95% of the defensive plays prior to the big game, was unexpectedly benched by Belichick and sat on the sidelines as the Patriots lost to the Philadelphia Eagles 41-33. After the game, Belichick did not elaborate on his decision, only stating that Butler's benching had nothing to do with disciplinary actions. Shortly after Super Bowl LII, Butler cut ties with the Patriots and signed with the Tennessee Titans as a free agent.

This is not the first time that Belichick has suddenly and inexplicably released key defensive players. He traded star players, Jamie Collins, linebacker, and Chandler Jones, defensive end – players that many people thought were indispensible to the team –and yet the next season, the Patriots were first in total defense for the league. It also didn't hurt the Patriots' winning record when Belichick cut defensive tackles, Vince Wilfork and Richard Seymour. One of Belichick's strategies is to trade his players before they start to decline and lose value, and before they start demanding costly contracts.

Belichick has learned to navigate his way around free agency. When unrestricted free agency began in 1992, the NFL encountered a lot of resistance from coaches, team owners, players, and fans about the new rules. The league was adamant; however, that unrestricted free agency would give teams a more competitive balance and stated that free agency offered a system that could be optimized. Belichick is one coach who quickly found ways to optimize the new free agency rules to his advantage.

Belichick has numerous ways in which to build his roster of players, from unrestricted free agency to the NFL draft, to trades and street free agents. To him, it doesn't matter how a player becomes a Patriot; it matters what they can bring to the playing field.

What Belichick is looking for in players are the qualities that have led Patriots' quarterback Tom Brady to become one of the most successful NFL quarterbacks in the history of the game. Although Brady certainly possesses raw talent, Belichick has stated in interviews with sports journalists that Brady wasn't born with natural athletic ability. His athletic achievement were acquired and developed over time. What Brady does have is a strong work ethic, focus, and intelligence.

Belichick expects his all of his players to work hard, in practice, in drills, in training, in meetings, and on game day. The athletes should devote their time and energies to perfecting their craft. This includes learning new workout techniques that can optimize outcome or experimenting with drills to improve performance. Belichick has witnessed the transformation of Tom Brady from an average player to a superman quarterback because of the hard work he puts in to his workouts and practices, and also from learning the mechanics of the game. Belichick looks for players who truly believe that they can become better and who push themselves to become so.

Focus is another trait that is highly valued by Belichick. He is looking for players with mental toughness and who remain entirely focused on the immediate goal. Football is a war that is won through a series of short battles. It is the ability to take one battle at a time and overcome the unique obstacles presented in that battle – ensuring victory before moving on to the next battle – that will win the war. Players should have the ability to block out next week's game so all their mental energies are dedicated to this week's game, the battle in the present. However, they should also be able to mentally move on from the previous battle and not let the previous week's performance affect this week's game. In football, that is a difficult thing to do. A defeat the previous week may dampen a team's morale and motivation. It may even break down teamwork and trust. On the other hand, a victory in last week's game may create overconfidence. A team that rests on its laurels is setting themselves up to be blindsided by a better prepared team. Belichick knows these things, which is why he emphasizes focus and staying in the moment to his players.

For Belichick, football is as much a mental game as it is a physical one. He has earned a reputation for filling his roster with smart players who have a mind for the game. He seeks out strategic thinkers and quick problem solvers. Football is often fast-paced, so players need to absorb and process a lot of information coming at them all at once and very quickly determine the best course of action. He wants players who can think proactively and reactively and who have vision. Above all, he wants a roster full of players who are not afraid to learn more…and who understand that they have more to learn. Belichick's football is a cerebral game and he wants the brains to back up the brawn.

PRINCIPLE 3: WE'RE ON TO…

When one football season ends, Bill Belichick doesn't waste time rehashing the previous year's successes and failures. Instead, he looks ahead. The new season means a renewal time…an opportunity to start fresh. In the age of free agency when player mobility is commonplace, it means that there is a degree of rebuilding each year as players leave and new ones join the team. As much as Belichick excels at coaching during game day, he is equally excellent at scouting and recruiting new talent and recruiting setting ambitious goals for the coming season. He once said, "Last year is last year," a pithy way for saying that he doesn't believe in resting on his laurels. HIs coaching philosophy includes approaching each season with fresh perspective. For a coach known for his consistent successes, it may come as a surprise that Belichick embraces change.

Of course, having a star quarterback like Tom Brady helps keep the victories coming. In fact, the consistent leadership of both Belichick and Brady is the driving force behind the successes that the New England Patriots have enjoyed. But Belichick and Brady are, perhaps, the only constant in an every-changing system.

Every year, the Patriots lose key players from their roster, yet the end results remains the same, or close to it. Eight Super Bowl appearances are proof of this. The team's successes are not negatively impacted by a changing roster. This is a testament to Belichick as a leader and coach, and to the winning system that he has put into place in New England. The wins are credited to the system, not to an individual, superstar player. Because of that, Belichick is able to fit new players into to replace departing ones without too many hiccups.

For example, following the Patriots' 2015 Super Bowl win over the Seattle Seahawks, Belichick lost five key players: defensive end Akeem Ayers, running back Shane Vereen, defensive tackle Vince Wilfork, and cornerbacks Brandon Browner and Darrelle Revis. The loss of just one of these players would have plunged any other team into a tailspin, but the Patriots were back on top, albeit with a vastly different-looking roster, just two seasons later when the New England Patriots again made it to the Super Bowl and clinched the championship with a 34-28 victory over the Atlanta Falcons. The continued successes of the franchise are possible because Belichick selects new players that can fit into the existing system and keep the winning machinery running smoothly. It is Belichick's knack for finding and developing the right talent to keep the victories coming.

It is clear that Belichik likes to win. Sports journalists frequently say Belichick has an addiction to winning, and there is a natural euphoria that accompanies victory that can spur one on to more successes. While it is true that success begets success, Belichick knows there is much more to the equation. As a keen observer and a student of the game, he has learned that winning comes as the result of many facets of the organization working together. He knows that his job as the head coach is to be cognizant of each of these facets so he can optimize each one. He needs to sweat the small stuff. Belichick is in a perpetual forward motion, always looking to push ahead and achieve the next win. He does not waste time or effort going backwards or dwelling on past defeats.

One of Belichick's fundamental principles is to view every loss as a learning opportunity. Losing is one of the best ways to improve because it forces one to re-examine their situation. In fact, Belichick has come to realize that one learns more from losses than they ever could from successes. Belichick's first head coaching position in Cleveland ended in a losing season and he was quickly out of a job. This failure would have been enough to keep a lesser coach from immediately jumping into another head coaching job. It would certainly be a jolt to one's self-confidence. But Belichick viewed it as a way to for him to improve himself mentally for the demands of being a head coach of a NFL team.

Losing is great motivation to work harder, be more prepared, and to evolve to fit changing conditions. Belichick agrees that winners are defined by the lessons they learn from failures. Losing is humbling, but it snaps one out of complacency. The true sign of a leader is one who takes responsibility for losses without assigning blame to others. Belichick allegedly apologized to his players following the Patriots' 17-14 loss to the New York Giants in Super Bowl XLII. He explained to them that his own lack of preparation was the reason for the loss and he took personal responsibility for the team's inability to finish their season undefeated.

That loss spurred Belichick on to re-evaluate his coaching methods. To maintain a culture of winning, Belichick understands that the system should be continuously refined and improved. No system can continue to be effective if it remains unchanged.

Bill Belichick grew up watching his father scout football players. When he began coaching himself, the younger Belichick developed an approach for evaluating potential players to determine their ability and how well they could adapt to his system. With the advent of free agency, he was forced to adapt his plan and tweak his approach. In fact, as the game of football evolves, so does Belichick, strive always to be at the cutting edge of changes within the NFL so that he can work the rules in his favor. Working with the rules, he found, is more effective and requires less energy than working against the system. His continuously-changing scouting and recruiting philosophy is instilled into every part of the Patriots' organization so that all aspects of the franchise are on the same page and all working together for the greater goal.

Belichick's obsession with winning is a result of his passion for the game of football. It is that passion that drives his coaching strategies. When he recruits and develops new talent, motivates and inspired existing players, and wrestles with all the small details within the Patriots' organization, it is because his love for the game of football is driving his competitive nature. He simply wants to win. He wants to be the best. He wants to keep learning and growing. He wants to develop new ways to overcome obstacles and solve problems that lay in his path to victory. And of equal importance, he wants players on his roster who are as passionate about the game of football as he is.

It is with passion that Belichick has immersed himself in his field. He focuses all his energies on improving his team, his players, and himself. For Belichick, there is no off-season. His obsession with being prepared is a year-round effort and a constant work-in-progress.

In the 2018 pre-season, Belichick is moving forward with his aggressive attack plan for the upcoming football season despite the loss of the Patriots' defensive coordinator, Matt Patricia, who left the New England franchise for the head coaching job with the Detroit Lions. Belichick is not worried. In fact, he is not rushing into filling the open position on the coaching staff. The chatter among the sports journalists following the story is that the current Patriots linebacker coach, Brian Flores, will be calling the plays from the sidelines come September, even though he has not had the title of defensive coordinator officially bestowed on him. At least, not yet.

Belichick is adopting a wait and see approach. He is assigning Patricia's duties to Flores and will observe the results before making the move permanent. Belichick has done this before and it has proven to be successful. Matt Patricia was not named the defensive coordinator until two years after Dean Pees depart the franchise in 2009. During that time, he served in an unofficial capacity, calling the defensive plays on the sidelines. It happened even earlier when Josh McDaniels took over from Charlie Weis when Weis left for the head coaching job at the University of Notre Dame.

Change is inevitable. Change is necessary to progress, as Belichick well knows. Whether it is a change in the players or a change in the coaching staff, Belichick approached change as opportunity. In football, there is no time for complacency or resting on one's laurels. Not when there are countless details that, when taken as a whole, could mean a few more points on the scoreboard on Sundays in the fall. These details, small as they may seem, add up to success. Belichick knows how to play the percentages to minimize risk and maximize outcome. He has shown that he is committed to doing what is needed to increase his team's chances of victory. This means playing an active role in all aspects of the franchise while putting his trust in his team of coaches and staff. It all adds up to a winning formula.

CONCLUSION

To the critics that say "football is only a game", it is important to remember that that "game" is a rich and vibrant part of American culture. It is more than a pastime. It is a deeply-rooted part of the American experience and one aspect of our shared cultural bond. Football creates subcultures of society, pockets of fans devoted to their team with a voracity we don't see among other sports. As Americans, we like winners. We enjoy seeing a coach build a team and motivate the player on a climb for the top. This is one reason why we like to watch the New England Patriots…it is like watching a master perfecting his art.

Bill Belichick has a unique approach to coaching that has led to his success. His key principles can easily be adapted to other leaders in other fields. Have passion for your job. Pick the right people to support you. Explore all avenues. Trust your team. Be prepared. Know what your enemy is doing and what they are capable of. Plan for every situation. Everything you do should support the end goal. While these principles have helped make Belichick one of the most successful NFL coaches of all time, they are also important life lessons that anyone can use.

Sports reporters like to talk about sports legacies, and, indeed, the when Belichick retires from coaching, he will leave a legacy behind. But football is a sport that breeds family legacies, with fathers and sons all involved in the game. Bill

Belichick is one layer of the Belichick football legacy. He learned the nuances of the game from his father, Steve Belichick, a successful football scout, and he has passed along his passion and knowledge to his own sons, both of whom have joined the Patriots organization. Brian Belichick is a defensive coaching assistant and Stephen Belichick is the safeties coach for New England. Clearly, the Belichick dynasty is going strong.

Football is big business. Today's coaches must juggle salary caps and personnel rules, all while developing a winning program that keep the fans coming in the gates on game day and the television sponsors happy. Belichick is a tycoon. He has proven himself to be an astute leader, a motivator of people, a bold strategist, and progressive thinker. At the New England Patriots keep amassing victories and garnering Super Bowl wins, it is hard to image how many more successes Belichick can achieve, but with his winning philosophy and passion for the sport, anything is possible.

In His Own Words
On Leadership

"You get the job done or you don't."

"Whatever success I've had it is because I've tried to understand the situation of the player. I think the coach's duty is to avoid complicating matters."

"I am who I am. In the end, I feel that what I'm accountable for is doing a good job as a football coach."

"There is an old saying about the strength of the wolf is the pack, and I think there is a lot of truth to that. On a football team, it's not the strength of the individual players, but it is the strength of the unit and how they all function together."

"There are no shortcuts to building a team each season. You build the foundation brick by brick."

"Tell me what the guy can do, don't tell me what he can't do, and we'll find a way to put that positive skill set in the defense and not ask him to be in a position where he can fail."

"You have to go with the person who you have the most confidence in, the most consistent. If it doesn't work, it doesn't work, but I'm going down with that person."

ON BEING TOTALLY PREPARED

"The only sign we have in the locker room is from 'The Art of War.' 'Every battle is won before it is fought."

"My personal coaching philosophy, my mentality, has always been to make things as difficult as possible for players in practice, however bad we can make them, I make them."

"Every game is an important game for us. Doesn't matter what's the next week – who we play, whether it's a bye week, Thanksgiving, Christmas, Halloween, Columbus Day. We don't care. We're just trying to go out there and win a game."

"You can play hard. You can play aggressive. You can give 120% but if one guy is out of position then someone is running through the line of scrimmage and he is going to gain a bunch of yards."

"I think a good quarterback or a good linebacker, a good safety, even though you have a lot of bodies moving out there, it slows down for them and they can really see it. Then there are other guys that it's a lot of guys moving and they don't see anything. It's like being at a busy intersection, just cars going everywhere. The guys that can really sort it out, they see the game at a slower pace and can really sort out and decipher all that movement, which is hard. But experience certainly helps that, yes."

"We have absolutely done as much work as we can on finding out things like that and we'll try to get all the information that we can as that would apply to any current situation, which I can't talk about."

"It's the business that you guys are in too. We try to get as much information as we can and make the best decisions that we can for the football team."

"You can't look back. We don't talk about last year. We don't talk about next week. We talk about today, and we talk about the next game. That's all we can really control."

ON A LACK OF TALENT CAN BE MADE UP FOR WITH HARD WORK

"Mental Toughness is doing the right thing for the team when it's not the best thing for you."

"Talent sets the floor, character sets the ceiling."

"The less versatile you are, the better you have to be at what you do well."

"I think everyone is a case-by-case basis. Whatever the circumstances are that come with any individual, they exist and you have to make a determination as to what your comfort level is with that person and the characteristics that they bring."

"I think a smart guy can learn. Some guys learn – it's just like all of us – some guys can learn electronics, some of us can't. Some people can learn something else, some of us can't. I mean, we're all wired differently."

"I'm not really worried about the other 31 teams."

"If you like football, and you like to come in and work on football, then the New England Patriots is a great place to be. If you don't, if it's a job, if you'd rather be doing something else, honestly you'd be better off with another team."

"I'm not on SnapFace and all those … I'm not too worried about what they put on InstantChat."

"If there is something that's your passion when you're young, do it. Let everything else take care of itself. Don't pick a career for money, or some other reason. Do what you love, because it will never feel like work."

"It is not all about talent. It's about dependability, consistency, being coachable, and understanding what you need to do to improve."

ON NEVER RESTING ON YOUR ACCOMPLISHMENTS

"If you sit back & spend too much time feeling good about what you did in the past, you're going to come up short next time."

"We'll continue to work hard to do a better job in every area going forward. I don't know where those little things will come from but we'll continue to be diligent on them."

"To live in the past is to die in the present."

"I think that we'll continue to try to look at ourselves in the mirror and see where we can do a better job, maybe where we can improve the process. But I think the fundamentals of the process will remain the same."

"We're always trying to do a better job on that and that's what we'll continue to do."

"You get the job done or you don't."

ON TEAM WORK

"On a team, it's not the strength of the individual players, but it is the strength of the unit and how they all function together."

"For a team to accomplish their goal, everybody's got to give up a little bit of their individuality."

"There are no shortcuts to building a team each season. You build the foundation brick by brick."

"You definitely go through a stage, most coaches do, where you see a good player and you get enamored, you really like what the player does, but then when you put him into your system, its not quite the same player that he was in another system. They have some strengths, but you can't utilize all of those strengths. If you try to utilize all of their strengths, you end up weakening a lot of the other players who are already in your system."

"I believe to have a championship team you want to have a championship team in every area, whether that's your starting quarterback, your strength coach, your medical staff, your area scouts, whatever it happens to be."

MORE FROM JACKSON CARTER BIOGRAPHIES

My goal is to spark the love of reading in young adults around the world. Too often children grow up thinking they hate reading because they are forced to read material they don't care about. To counter this we offer accessible, easy to read biographies about sportspeople that will give young adults the chance to fall in love with reading.

Go to the Website Below to Join Our Community

https://mailchi.mp/7cced1339ff6/jcbcommunity

Or Find Us on Facebook at

www.facebook.com/JacksonCarterBiographies

As a Member of Our Community You Will Receive:

First Notice of Newly Published Titles

Exclusive Discounts and Offers

Influence on the Next Book Topics

Don't miss out, join today and help spread the love of reading around the world!

OTHER WORKS BY JACKSON CARTER BIOGRAPHIES

Made in the USA
Middletown, DE
19 April 2020